W9-AWQ-800

201 Thematic Riddle Poems to Build Literacy

Short, Irresistible, Guess-Me Poems
Perfect for Shared Reading, Circle Time,
and More!

by Betsy Franco

SCHOLASTIC
PROFESSIONAL BOOKS

New York • Toronto • London • Auckland • Sydney
Mexico City • New Delhi • Hong Kong

Dedication

For my Uncle Sam who played
imaginary games with me

Scholastic Inc. grants teachers permission to photocopy the content of this book for classroom use only.
No other part of this publication may be reproduced in whole or in part, or stored in a retrieval system,
or transmitted in any form or by any means, electronic, mechanical, photocopying, recording, or otherwise,
without written permission of the publisher. For information regarding permission, write to
Scholastic Inc., 555 Broadway, New York, NY 10012.

Cover design by Norma Ortiz
Cover artwork by Cheryl Phelps
Interior artwork by Jane A. Dippold
Interior design by Sydney Wright

ISBN: 0-439-13121-9
Copyright © 2000 by Betsy Franco
All rights reserved.
Printed in the U.S.A.

Contents

Science

Letters and Numbers

All Sorts of Animals

At School

Interesting Animals

Calendar and Seasons

Introduction

What sort of poetry is timeless, fun, and packed with learning? Take a guess! Riddle poems, of course!

Riddles are one of the oldest forms of poetry for a good reason. They make us grin! They make us think!

Sharing riddles:
* Builds key literacy skills
* Strengthens higher-level thinking skills
* Captures and focuses student attention
* Enriches thematic units
* Adds fun to every lesson!

201 Thematic Riddle Poems to Build Literacy will benefit your teaching in many ways. Here are just a few ideas for putting them to work in your classroom:

Inspire students during shared-reading time. Copy riddle poems onto chart paper and turn your emergent readers into reading-time helpers. The kids will feel proud to use your teacher's pointer to model how to read from left to right, point out helpful words in the riddle, and identify initial consonants. Ask, *Which words are clues to solve the*

riddle? You'll observe kids supporting one another's learning.

Enliven morning meetings with easy-to-read riddles in pocket charts. Simply write the riddles on sentence strips and tuck them in each pocket. Write and/or illustrate the answers on index cards and slip them in, too.

Excite students with creative, interactive bulletin-board displays. Staple large manila envelopes onto a bulletin board. Write one riddle on the front of each envelope. Then tuck the answers inside each corresponding envelope. In order to encourage kids to use the riddle bulletin board effectively, introduce it to the class. Invite a pair of kids to be bulletin board helpers. Have each child read aloud one riddle from the bulletin board to the class. As a whole class, discuss which words in the riddle are clues to the answer. Then say to each helper: *Read us the answer from the envelope, please!* Help children build self-confidence in riddle solving by inviting them to visit the bulletin board in their free time. Keep the riddle poems fresh and engaging with selections from *201 Thematic Riddle Poems*.

Encourage hands-on learning with riddle poems represented on finger-friendly flannel boards. Copy riddle poems and answers onto colorful sentence strips. Place Velcro™ on the back and stick. Kids can match riddle poems with riddle solutions. Your students will enjoy this multisensory treat. And you'll hear them read with confidence.

Build oral literacy during transition times. Turn transition times into exciting language-learning times. If you're studying colors, read selections from *Which Mystery Color?* (14) and *Which Stoplight Colors?* (18). Use lively color riddles to motivate kids to form a line, visit the library, prepare for a field trip, or just get ready for a snack. Say, *If you are wearing the answer to this*

riddle on your shirt, raise your hand! Choose a child whose hand is raised to state the riddle's answer. Then invite the other children who are wearing that particular color to join the group. Continue the process until everybody has joined the group. This flexible format extends oral literacy and makes class management fun!

Delight students with collaborative riddle books. Invite each child to choose a favorite riddle from *201 Thematic Riddle Poems*. Give each child a piece of plain white paper on which to copy the riddle and draw a related picture. Laminate the student-created pages and three-hole-punch their left edges. Then link them together with brass fasteners to assemble a special class book. Celebrate poetry by inviting students to share their favorite riddle poems with the whole class. Then give your collaborative book a place of honor in your classroom library.

Invigorate your learning centers with riddles on audiotape. Kids will love to hear themselves reading, and you'll love having authentic assessments. Add audiotapes to student portfolios. Help kids hear how they've improved their reading fluency. Play the tapes at parent-teacher conferences. Tapes enable parents to listen to their child read and actually hear what their child is learning in your classroom. Document student development and reinforce emerging literacy with kids reading on tape. Make the most of an essential assessment tool in your PreK–2 classroom.

Instant Ideas for Using Riddles

Add rhythm and rhyme to every aspect of your emergent literacy program with the playful riddles and activities in this book. The following pages cover some of the ways these cross-curricular riddles will add fun and flavor to your classroom instruction!

Refresh Thematic Units

Enliven your thematic units with rhyming riddle activities. If your theme is colors, for example, choose selections from *Which Mystery Color?* (14), *Which Colorful Fruit or Veggie?* (17), and *Which Stoplight Color?* (18)! Are poems about school more appropriate for you? Then share selections from *What Can You Find in the Classroom?* (53), *What Am I Playing?* (55), and *Balls: Which Sport?* (56). Let *201 Thematic Riddle Poems* jump-start your thematic unit with poems that will delight emergent readers.

> ### Which Shape am I?
> A bathroom tile,
> a checkerboard game—
> my four straight sides
> are all the same!
> I'm a _____.
>
> **Answer: square**

Let's Practice!

If you want to add zip to your thematic unit on shapes, read selections from *Which Shape Am I?* (19). Teach your students to recognize shapes and the words that name them. Reinforce the concept that words denote meaning. By offering both printed words and paper shapes, children at different language-learning levels will be able to participate with relative ease.

★ Make paper cutouts of basic shapes, providing kids with concrete examples of word meaning. Print the shapes' names on index cards.

★ Put the shapes and word cards on your chalkboard ledge.

★ Ask the class, *Which shape or which word is "circle"?* Invite one child at a time to select either a shape or a word card. After each child's correct choice, repeat the word aloud and show the corresponding shape. *This is the square shape. And this is the word "square"!*

Not only will this exercise reinforce children's knowledge of shapes, but it will also help them build important connections between written and oral language. Use it at *circle* time! What better time to study shapes?

Build Essential Phonics Skills

Help children construct knowledge about letter sound/symbol relationships. Invite them to listen for initial consonants with riddles from *Which Letter?* (40) Focus your lesson on hearing initial consonant sounds.

Which Letter?

This letter of the alphabet
is in *some messy* words you know,
like *mucky, muddy, mopping, milk.*
Now write some other words below!

Answer: Mm

Let's Practice!

The same initial sound appears in *messy, mucky, muddy, mopping,* and *milk.*

★ Read the poem together. Tell your students, *Say the sound your ears hear the most.*

★ Invite children to think of other words that begin with the same sound by asking, *What first sound does this group of words share?*

★ Brainstorm more words that begin with the same sound. Write the words students generate on chart paper, creating a word bank of Mm words. As you encounter more Mm words in literature, add those to your list!

•**Variation:** Encourage children to use words from the Mm word bank to compose stories. Each time a word in their stories begins with Mm, have your students underline it. Invite students to read their stories from your classroom's author chair. Celebrate literacy at every turn!

Teach Rhyming Word Families

Teaching emergent readers to recognize that many words rhyme introduces them to the important concept of word families.

Which Pet Do You Pick?

I swim in water all day long.
You feed me little flakes.
If I were wild and not a pet,
I'd live in streams and lakes.
Pick a pet.

Answer: fish

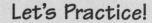

Let's Practice!

Capture your students' attention with transparencies. Roll that overhead projector out from the closet. It's an incredibly powerful teaching tool!

★ Choose a rhyming riddle from *201 Thematic Riddle Poems*. Use permanent marker to copy it onto an overhead transparency.

★ Project the transparency onto your wall screen. As your students read along with you, encourage them to listen to the sounds that combine to create words.

★ Ask your students to identify the rhyming words. *How are the endings of these words similar? What **rime** do they share?* Highlight the rhyming words on the transparency with a bold-colored marker.

★ Use chart paper to record word families. Whenever you encounter more words with the same **rime**, add them to the word bank!

Please note: You'll notice words that rhyme are not always members of the same word family.

Enhance Critical-Thinking Skills

Playful rhymes provide a comfortable, low-stress setting for creative problem solving. Invite children to use word clues to construct an answer. By providing clue words, riddles invite kids to make educated guesses. Help your students be riddle detectives! Ask,

Which words are helpful clues to solve this riddle poem? Be sure to discuss any riddle poems that seem especially challenging for your students to solve.

Who's Hatching?
They are skinny and long
curled up in their eggs.
Then they slither right out
with no arms and no legs.
Who's hatching? _____

Answer: snakes

Let's Practice!

★ Cut an oval egg shape out of colored paper and rest it on your chalkboard ledge.

★ Write a riddle on the board from the selection titled *Who's Hatching?* (57) Cover the riddle's answer with the paper egg so that the children can't see it.

★ Read the poem aloud to your class. Then ask, *Who's hatching?* Lift the egg to show the answer. Have students support their answers with clue words from the riddle.

•**Variation:** Break the class into a few mixed-level groups. Provide each group with several poems to solve from *201 Thematic Riddle Poems*. When each group has completed the activity, meet as a whole class to share riddles and answers.

TEACHER TIP!

Mega-Fun Technology Tips

Add a high-tech dimension to learning with riddles. Use your classroom computer to reinforce language arts skills and introduce new ones in inspiring ways.

Improve Reading & Writing Skills

▲ Invite older kids to use word-processing software to set some of these riddles in type. Ask students to identify rhyming words with boldface.

▲ Develop a class book of original riddles. Invite students to write riddles and then to illustrate them with drawing software.

Cultivate Listening & Speaking Skills

▲ Celebrate reading by recording some of the *201 Thematic Riddle Poems* on audiotapes. Put them in your listening center, where kids can read and listen to their best-loved riddles.

▲ Create a class videotape of your students reading their favorite riddles aloud. Share it with parents at open house!

Make Pocket Chart Learning More Meaningful

Pocket charts are versatile and valuable teaching tools. Use them to reinforce a lesson, enliven a Read Aloud, or enhance a Guided Reading experience. A pocket chart is essentially a sturdy wall chart with places to insert words, pictures, and sentences. Most have ten rows of transparent plastic pockets that readily provide a generic framework for poetry, songs, and literature. Pocket charts make building literacy hands-on and minds-on! Use them with your students to link text to pictures, match words that rhyme, and much more!

Which Season?

In _____,
trees <u>are nice and bare</u>.
and <u>gray's the color of the sky</u>.
We like to <u>play in the snow</u> all day.
We like the _____, you and I.
Which season?

Answer: winter

Let's Practice!

Using a Pocket Chart Is as Easy as 1–2–3!

Riddle poems in pocket charts add pizzazz to your language arts program.

★ Enjoy the poem at left year-round (62). Copy its generic text onto white sentence strips. Then tuck them into the rows of your pocket chart.

★ Write the words *spring, summer, winter,* and *autumn* on strips of the same color paper. Put them, in no particular order, in an empty pocket towards the bottom of the chart.

★ Write the phrases that describe winter on sentence strips of another color. Tuck them in the spaces of your riddle's framework. Now you're ready to share the poem with your class. It's that easy!

• **Variation:**

Writing new versions of a riddle is a good method for exploring descriptive language! Place the framework on the pocket chart with a seasonal word tucked in the uppermost row. Ask, *What phrases describe this season?* You'll start a seasonal brainstorm! Write the student-generated phrases on sentence strips and insert them in your generic framework. You've created a riddle innovation!

Connecting Reading With Math and Science

Math and Science are everywhere. You'll find them embedded in *Colors and Shapes, Farm* *Animals, Me, Popular Animals, Letters and Numbers, All Sorts of Animals, Interesting Animals, Calendar and Seasons,* and *Science,* of course. Revisit the Table of Contents pages (3–4) for a breakdown of all the riddles in this book. Put riddles to work for you. They're an instant way of bridging the gap between language arts and other content areas.

How Many?

Add <u>2</u> plus <u>3</u>
and every time
your answer will be me,
no matter if you're adding
frogs or wild chimpanzees.

Answer: 5

Boost student understanding of number concepts with simple story problems from *How Many?* (47) This activity works well in small groups.

★ Write the riddle poem on the chalkboard or dry-erase board. Write each of the numbers 1 to 10 on index cards. Place the number cards on your board's ledge, in no particular order.

★ Invite your students to fill in any two numbers in the blanks to create a simple story problem. Read the riddle aloud.

★ Ask the kids to write the problem on paper. Ask, *Which mathematical operation did you need to use? Addition? Subtraction?*

★ Solve the problem on the board. Encourage good study habits by asking, *How can we check our work?* On the board, write the problem presented by the riddle: 2 + 3 = 5.

TEACHER TIP!

Boost ESL Fluency With Skill-Building Riddle Poems

▲ Provide "hint tickets" on index cards. Each card indicates the answer's first or last letter.

▲ Write several possible riddle responses on a dry-erase board. Reluctant writers will readily join the fun if they have choices. Invite children to fill in the circle that corresponds to the poem's solution, familiarizing them with standardized-test formats!

▲ Offer illustrations and photographs as answer choices. Students who use oral-language comprehension will choose the picture or photo that best represents the riddle's solution.

Extending Learning With Riddle Innovations

Children love to create their own rhymes, especially riddles. Make the most of the riddles in this book by using their different structures as a springboard and a model for writing. Ask your students what they notice about riddles. *What do these riddles have in common?*

Ask students to try these ideas when they're constructing riddles:

★ Name the subject of their poem indirectly.

★ Supply specific and vivid clues.

★ Challenge the reader to solve the riddle.

★ Assume the persona of the mystery subject.

★ Provide clues through an unidentified *voice.*

Which Letter?

This letter of the alphabet
is in some <u>silly</u> words you know,
like <u>slurp</u> and <u>slug</u> and <u>slip</u> and <u>slide</u>.
Now write some other words below!

Answer: Ss

surprising   serious   super

Let's Practice!

You're ready to write riddle innovations.

★ Separate your class into a few mixed-level groups for this activity.

★ Invite each group of students to brainstorm alternate words for the poem. Insert those new words in place of *silly* and *slurp, slug, slip,* and *slide.* For 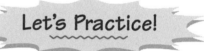 example, *silly* can become *surprising* or *serious* or *super.*

★ Ask children to develop their own riddle poem innovations with the support of their small groups. When everybody has rewritten one riddle, encourage your emergent writers to share their writing with the class, peers, and family.

• **Variation:** If your students liked writing innovations, they'll love writing original riddles. Remind them to think about the structure of their favorite riddles from this book. Read aloud several excerpts from *201 Thematic Riddle Poems* with your students, including the riddle at left. Ask, *What makes a riddle . . . a riddle?* And remember, a riddle poem does not need to rhyme to be considered a riddle. Writing in rhyme may be a daunting task for young writers.

Which Mystery Color?

Cherries, apples, pomegranates,
ladybugs, and roses.
At circus time, the clowns all wear
this color for their noses.
Name the mystery color. _____

Answer: red

It's the darkest dark
of the sky at night.
It's the color you see
with your eyes shut tight.
Name the mystery color. _____

Answer: black

On American flags
both old and new,
There's red and there's white
and there's this color, too.
Name the mystery color. _____

Answer: blue

The color of a daffodil
that's growing in the sun,
or a bunch of eight bananas
that are ripening one by one.
Name the mystery color. _____

Answer: yellow

The color from mixing
red and blue
is the color of plums
and grape juice, too.
Name the mystery color. _____

Answer: purple

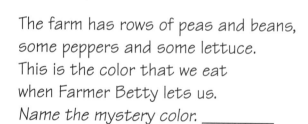

The farm has rows of peas and beans,
some peppers and some lettuce.
This is the color that we eat
when Farmer Betty lets us.
Name the mystery color. _____

Answer: green

It's a pumpkin in the autumn,
ripe and golden in the light.
It's a jack-o-lantern's face,
bright and scary in the night.
Name the mystery color. _____

Answer: orange

I see this color
all around
as snowflakes float
down to the ground.
Name the mystery color. _____

Answer: white

What color is a robin's song?
What color is a breeze?
What color is the buzzing
of a busy honeybee?
Name the mystery color. _____

Answer: any color you choose

Which Colorful Fruit or Veggie?

Outside I'm green.
I'm pink inside,
where all my little
black seeds hide.
Which fruit is it? _____

Answer: watermelon

I'm bright, bright orange with green on top.
The sound I make is *crunch*
whenever you eat me as a snack
or munch me in your lunch.
Which veggie is it? _____

Answer: carrot

I come in red and yellow.
I also can be green.
I may be the home of a hungry worm,
so make sure I am clean.
Which fruit is it? _____

Answer: apple

With all my eyes I still can't see.
I grow down underneath the ground.
You eat me whole or cut me thin
and fry me till I'm golden brown.
Which veggie is it? _____

Answer: potato

Which Stoplight Color?

Ladybug in
the flower bed
didn't cross
when the light turned _____.

Answer: red

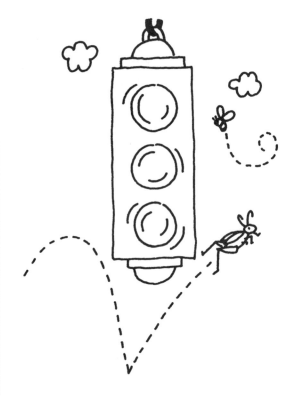

Bee, who's such
a busy fellow,
waited to cross
when the light turned _____.

Answer: yellow

Grasshopper hopping
in the beans
crossed the street
when the light turned _____.

Answer: green

Which Shape Am I?

A pizza, a clock,
a bicycle wheel—
I have no sides,
but I'm for real.
I'm a _____.

Answer: circle

A door, a book,
a tabletop—
four corners wait
where my four sides stop.
I'm a _____.

Answer: rectangle

An arrowhead,
a party hat—
I've got three sides.
Now think of that.
I'm a _____.

Answer: triangle

A bathroom tile,
a checkerboard game—
my four straight sides
are all the same!
I'm a _____.

Answer: square

Who's Down on the Farm?

He cock-a-doodles
on the farm.
He is the farmer's
loud alarm.
Who is he? _____

Answer: rooster

Her baby's called a little lamb.
Her coat is soft and white.
The farmer cuts her wool each year.
It keeps you warm at night!
Who is she? _____

Answer: sheep

He has a very wobbly chin.
His wings flap up and down.
Thanksgiving Day, he'd fly away,
but he's stuck on the ground.
Who is he? _____

Answer: turkey

She chews her cud.
She softly moos.
Her fresh white milk's
her gift to you.
Who is she? _____

Answer: cow

He barks and runs around a lot
to herd the sheep together.
He keeps the farmer company
in every kind of weather.
Who is he? _____

Answer: sheep dog

Paddle, paddle, paddle.
Dive, dive, dive.
Quack, quack, quack.
It's good to be alive!
Who is she? _____

Answer: duck

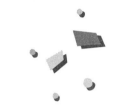

He hoots and hoots in the barn at night.
He catches lots of mice.
He turns his head this way and that
and blinks his two large eyes.
Who is he? _____

Answer: barn owl

Clippity clop, clippity clop.
She lifts her head to neigh.
She's trotting to the big red barn
to eat some fresh-cut hay.
Who is she? _____

Answer: horse

Who's Being Fed?

Someone on the farm today
was happy to be fed.

_____, _____, _____, _____

is what that someone said.
So tell me, who was fed?

Answers will vary.

Try these sounds in the blanks:
sheep: *baa, baa, baa, baa*
duck: *quack, quack, quack, quack*
pig: *oink, oink, oink, oink*
rooster: *cock-a-doodle-doo*
goose: *honk, honk, honk, honk*
goat: *naa, naa, naa, naa*
cat: *meow, meow, meow, meow*
horse: *neigh, neigh, neigh, neigh*
cow: *moo, moo, moo, moo*
chick: *cheep, cheep, cheep, cheep*
chicken: *cluck, cluck, cluck, cluck*
dog: *woof, woof, woof, woof*
turkey: *gobble, gobble, gobble, gobble*

Which of the Five Senses?

A cricket does this with its leg.
I do it with my ears.
I do it when a siren sounds
or people scream and cheer.
What do I do? _____

Answer: hear

A bat can use its ears for this.
I do it with my eyes.
I do it when I look at a bird
or watch a full moon rise.
What do I do? _____

Answer: see

A boa does this with its tongue,
I do it with my nose.
If someone's baking cookie dough,
then I am sure to know.
What do I do? _____

Answer: smell

A cat has whiskers just for this.
I do it with my hands.
I do it when I pat a dog
or feel the silky sand.
What do I do? _____

Answer: touch

An eel does this with its skin,
a housefly with its feet.
I do this with my mouth each day
when I sit down to eat.
What do I do? _____

Answer: taste

Which Part of Me?

They're perfect for batting,
and that's not all!
They each have an elbow
for throwing a ball.
Which part of me? _____

Answer: my arms

I use them when I kick a ball.
They take me where I want to go.
They fit inside my socks and shoes.
I use them standing tippy-toe.
Which part of me? _____

Answer: my feet

I use them when I run and jump.
They help me when I skip a rope.
They both have knees that help me bend.
You'll guess this part of me, I hope.
Which part of me? _____

Answer: my legs

I use them to eat. I use them to clap.
I use them to point and to write.
I use them to paint and to brush my hair.
I use them to fly a kite!
Which part of me? _____

Answer: my hands

This part of me
can wear a hat
and wink and smell
and hear and chat.
Which part of me? _____

Answer: my head

All ten of them get wrinkled
when I'm sitting in the tub,
and if I trip on something,
then one of them gets stubbed.
Which part of me? _____

Answer: my toes

How Do I Feel?

When someone hurts my feelings,
or a good friend moves away,
I start to feel pretty _____.
The world looks kind of gray.
How do I feel? _____

Answer: sad

Whenever it's my birthday,
or when Grandma brings us treats,
I get a _____ feeling
that's warm inside of me.
How do I feel? _____

Answer: happy

When someone breaks my favorite things
or calls me yucky names,
then I feel very _____.
It's kind of like a flame.
How do I feel? _____

Answer: angry

When my friends yell, "Happy birthday!"
and I can't believe my eyes,
then I get this special feeling,
and that feeling is _____.

Answer: surprised

What Makes Us Special?

My Name

No matter what I say or do,
my name will always be the same.
It starts with ___
and ends with ___.
Now count to 3 and say my name. _____

Answers will vary.

My Friend

Friends at home,
friends at school,
friends both old and new.
I have a friend with _____
(example: long brown hair or a yellow shirt)
My friend is next to you!

Answers will vary.

Someone in the Classroom

There's someone in the classroom.
It's one of all of you.
I'll tell you what s/he likes to do
and that will be the clue.
S/he likes to _____.
(example: play on the swings)
So now can you guess who? _____

Answers will vary.

• **Variation:** Tuck kids' photos in your pocket chart backward after *So now can you guess who?* When you
read the riddle together, invite one child to flip the photograph around to see his/her classmate!
Hint: Laminate photos to make them last all year!

Which Favorite Toy?

He sits on my bed
with his brown furry hair
and his paws without claws.
He's my old _____ _____.

Answer: teddy bear

Hear it flapping in the wind.
Watch as it takes flight.
Run around so it stays up.
This toy is called a _____.

Answer: kite

Its string is quite long.
It spins high and low.
It twirls up and down.
It's called a _____.

Answer: yo-yo

I'm blowing balls into the air,
but they can get in trouble.
They stop and pop on anything sharp.
You guessed! I'm blowing _____.

Answer: bubbles

I Spy: Which Animal?

I spy with my little eye
a mammal with a spout.
It's bigger than my grandma's car.
It swims to get about.
I spy a _____.

Answer: whale

I spy with my little eye
a mammal's big brown jaws.
It lives in caves and hibernates.
It fishes with its paws.
I spy a _____.

Answer: bear

I spy with my little eye
a bird that "wears a suit."
It's black and white.
It slides on ice. It's really very cute.
I spy a _____.

Answer: penguin

I spy with my little eye
a creature sleeping upside down.
It sleeps in dark and spooky caves.
On Halloween it flies around.
I spy a _____.

Answer: bat

What Kind of Bear?

Hear me growl my growl.
See my brown, brown hair.
I hibernate in winter.
I'm a furry _____ bear.

Answer: grizzly

Hear me growl my growl.
See my black, black hair.
I hibernate in winter.
I'm a furry, big _____ bear.

Answer: black

Hear me growl my growl.
See my white, white hair.
I'm not the hibernating kind.
I'm a furry _____ bear.

Answer: polar

What Do You Know About Penguins?

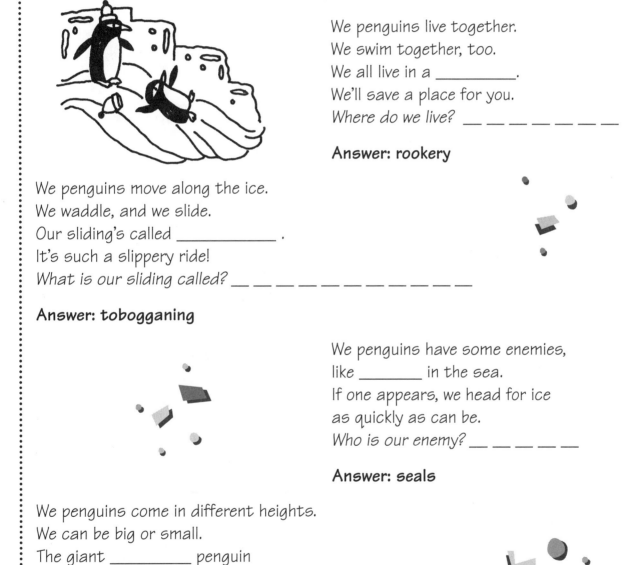

We penguins live together.
We swim together, too.
We all live in a _____.
We'll save a place for you.
Where do we live? __ __ __ __ __ __ __

Answer: rookery

We penguins move along the ice.
We waddle, and we slide.
Our sliding's called _____ .
It's such a slippery ride!
What is our sliding called? __ __ __ __ __ __ __ __ __ __ __

Answer: tobogganing

We penguins have some enemies,
like _____ in the sea.
If one appears, we head for ice
as quickly as can be.
Who is our enemy? __ __ __ __ __

Answer: seals

We penguins come in different heights.
We can be big or small.
The giant _____ penguin
is the biggest one of all.
Which is the biggest penguin? __ __ __ __ __ __ __

Answer: emperor

Which Whale?

The h_____ whale
is known for its song.
The b_____ whale is famous
because it is so long.

Answers: humpback, blue

A k_____ whale's mouth
has some sharp teeth in there.
It uses its spout
when it comes up for air.

Answer: killer

The s_____ whale
has a "pushed-in" snout.
It moves its fluke
to swim about.

Answer: sperm

Which Community Worker Am I?

Fire! Fire!
9-1-1!
I fight the blaze
until it's done.
Who am I? _____

Answer: firefighter

I get up early
just to bake
your cookies, rolls,
and bread and cake.
Who am I? _____

Answer: baker

In rain or snow
or sun or hail,
I walk to your homes
to deliver the mail.
Who am I? _____

Answer: mail carrier

Stitches and itches,
slips and falls,
colds and flu—
I fix them all.
Who am I? _____

Answer: doctor

I'm there for you
both night and day
so you are safe
at school and play.
Who am I? _____

Answer: police officer

Math and reading,
science, too.
I teach these things
to all of you.
Who am I? _____

Answer: teacher

Let me help you
find a book
on bears or bees
or how to cook.
Who am I? _____

Answer: librarian

Transportation: Which Kind?

"All Aboard!"
Clackity-clack.
We go speeding
down the track.
What is it? _____

Answer: train

With seat belts on,
we drive around.
We stop and go
all over town.
What is it? _____

Answer: car

The pilot takes us
up so high—
a giant "bird"
up in the sky.
What is it? _____

Answer: airplane

Up in the sky,
above the clouds,
propeller whirring
fast and loud.
What is it? _____

Answer: helicopter

Across the lake
I row and row.
The harder I pull,
the faster I go.
What is it? _____

Answer: rowboat

Flap, flap, flap,
Wind in the sails.
Waves in our faces.
Time to bail!
What is it? _____

Answer: sailboat

Pedals twirl
and wheels turn.
We ride to school
and then return.
*What is it?*_____

Answer: bicycle

What's the Weather Report?

In winter when it falls on you,
you always look surprised.
But when you try to catch it,
it melts before your eyes.
What's falling? _____

Answer: snow

It can steal your hat.
It can blow your hair.
It can make the leaves
dance here and there.
What's blowing? _____

Answer: wind

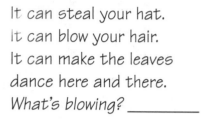

It *pitter-patters* on the roof.
It waters garden flowers.
When we go out without a coat,
it gives us all a shower.
What's coming down? _____

Answer: rain

Puffy white pillows
fill the sky.
They hold the rain
way up so high.
What's up there? _____

Answer: clouds

Rumble, rumble,
boom, boom, boom!
Dazzling light
fills up the room!
*What's happening?*_____

Answer: thunder and lightning

What Will I Wear in This Weather?

To keep my hands warm
when building in snow,
my m_____ go with me
wherever I go.
What go with me? _____

Answer: mittens

I put on my r_____
and pull on the hood.
Whenever it's raining,
my r_____ feels good.
What do I put on? _____

Answer: raincoat

Whenever it's sunny,
I pull on my sh_____.
I wear them to school
and for all kinds of sports.
What do I put on? _____

Answer: shorts

On windy days,
I hold my _____,
or off my head
it flies like that.
What do I hold? _____

Answer: hat

Sky: What's Shining?

Sometimes it's small, sometimes it's big.
It shines at night way out in space.
It seems to follow you around.
Some people say it has a face.
What's shining? _____

Answer: moon

First one comes out, then thousands more.
Some people wish on them at night.
They form the pictures in the sky.
They make a very twinkly sight.
What's shining? _____

Answer: stars

It rises each morning and stays in the sky
till it's nighttime, and then it must go.
It shines on the flowers and gardens and trees.
They need it in order to grow.
What's shining? _____

Answer: sun

There are nine of them,
and earth is one.
They orbit round
and round the sun.
What's shining? _____

Answer: planets

Which Letter?

This letter of the alphabet
is in some <u>awesome</u> words you know,
like <u>alligator</u>, <u>ant</u>, <u>afraid</u>.
Now write some other words below!

Answer: Aa

This letter of the alphabet
is in some <u>beautiful</u> words you know,
like <u>bubble</u>, <u>bunny</u>, <u>butterfly</u>.
Now write some other words below!

Answer: Bb

This letter of the alphabet
is in some <u>cool</u> words you know,
like <u>cactus</u>, <u>cake</u>, and <u>cottontail</u>.
Now write some other words below!

Answer: Cc

This letter of the alphabet
is in some <u>dandy</u> words you know,
like <u>dolphin</u>, <u>duck</u>, and <u>dinosaur</u>.
Now write some other words below!

Answer: Dd

This letter of the alphabet
is in some <u>easy</u> words you know,
like <u>eat</u> and <u>egg</u> and even <u>eyes</u>.
Now write some other words below!

Answer: Ee

This letter of the alphabet
is in some <u>funny</u> words you know,
like <u>feather</u>, <u>fast</u>, and <u>fiddler crab</u>.
Now write some other words below!

Answer: Ff

This letter of the alphabet
is in some <u>good old</u> words you know,
like <u>garden</u>, <u>growing</u>, <u>green</u>, and <u>give</u>.
Now write some other words below!

Answer: Gg

This letter of the alphabet
is in some <u>happy</u> words you know,
like <u>howdy</u>, <u>hi</u>, and <u>Halloween</u>.
Now write some other words below!

Answer: Hh

This letter of the alphabet
is in some <u>interesting</u> words you know,
like <u>igloo</u>, <u>itch</u>, and <u>ice-cream cone</u>.
Now write some other words below!

Answer: Ii

This letter of the alphabet
is in some <u>jazzy</u> words you know,
like <u>joke</u> and <u>jeep</u> and <u>jump</u> and <u>jig</u>.
Now write some other words below!

Answer: Jj

This letter of the alphabet
is in some <u>king-size</u> words you know,
like <u>kindergarten</u> and <u>kangaroo</u>.
Now write some other words below!

Answer: Kk

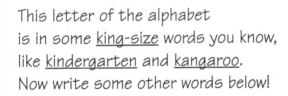

This letter of the alphabet
is in some <u>lively</u> words you know,
like <u>leap</u> and <u>laugh</u> and <u>lightning bug</u>.
Now write some other words below!

Answer: Ll

This letter of the alphabet
is in some <u>messy</u> words you know,
like <u>mucky</u>, <u>muddy</u>, <u>mopping</u>, <u>milk</u>.
Now write some other words below!

Answer: Mm

This letter of the alphabet
is in some <u>nifty</u> words you know,
like <u>nice</u> and <u>nothing</u>, <u>night</u> and <u>newt</u>.
Now write some other words below!

Answer: Nn

This letter of the alphabet
is in <u>outstanding</u> words you know,
like <u>open</u>, <u>old</u>, <u>okay</u>, and <u>orange</u>.
Now write some other words below!

Answer: Oo

This letter of the alphabet
is in some <u>playful</u> words you know,
like <u>pizza</u>, <u>pollywog</u>, and <u>pop</u>.
Now write some other words below!

Answer: Pp

This letter of the alphabet
is in <u>quite</u> a lot of words you know,
like <u>quick</u> and <u>quack</u> and <u>quilt</u> and <u>queen</u>.
Now write some other words below!

Answer: Qq

This letter of the alphabet
is in <u>rip-roaring</u> words you know,
like <u>race</u> and <u>ran</u> and <u>ride</u> and <u>riddle</u>.
Now write some other words below!

Answer: Rr

This letter of the alphabet
is in some <u>silly</u> words you know,
like <u>slurp</u> and <u>slug</u> and <u>slip</u> and <u>slide</u>.
Now write some other words below!

Answer: Ss

This letter of the alphabet
is in some <u>tiny</u> words you know,
like <u>to</u> and <u>two</u> and <u>tip</u> and <u>top</u>.
Now write some other words below!

Answer: Tt

This letter of the alphabet
is in some <u>unusual</u> words you know,
like <u>underwear</u> and <u>upside down</u>.
Now write some other words below!

Answer: Uu

This letter of the alphabet
is in some <u>very nice</u> words you know,
like <u>velvet</u>, <u>vest</u>, and <u>valentine</u>.
Now write some other words below!

Answer: Vv

This letter of the alphabet
is in some <u>wonderful</u> words you know,
like <u>wiggle</u>, <u>wild</u>, and <u>waterfall</u>.
Now write some other words below!

Answer: Ww

This letter of the alphabet
is in <u>extraordinary</u> words you know,
like <u>x-ray</u>, <u>exit</u>, <u>excellent</u>.
Now write some other words below!

Answer: Xx

This letter of the alphabet
is in some <u>yummy</u> words you know,
like <u>yogurt</u>, <u>yam</u>, and <u>yellow</u> cake.
Now write some other words below!

Answer: Yy

This letter of the alphabet
is in some <u>zippy</u> words you know,
like <u>zigzag</u>, <u>zipper</u>, <u>zip</u>, and <u>zap</u>.
Now write some other words below!

Answer: Zz

How Many?

____ little ladybugs
pretty as can be.
____ flew down and
landed on me.
How many ladybugs
left in the tree?

Answers will vary.

Take the numbers ____ and ____. (Insert two numbers.)
I'm somewhere in between those two.
They say I'm _____. (odd or even)
So who am I?
Just use the clues I gave to you.

Answers will vary.

Add ____ plus ____
and every time,
your answer will be me,
no matter if you're adding
frogs or wild chimpanzees.

Answers will vary.

Can You Bee a Bug Detective?

I have 5 eyes,
2 pairs of wings,
3 body parts,
and other things.
But most of all
I jump so far,
when it comes to my hop,
I'm a superstar.
Bee a bug detective. _____

Answer: grasshopper

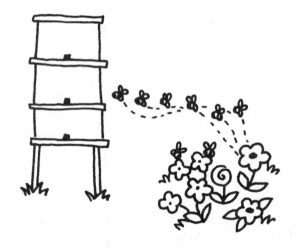

I always wear a crimson coat
with dots on either side.
I fly away if I get scared.
It's hard for me to hide.
Bee a bug detective. _____

Answer: ladybug

Please come to our house for the afternoon,
and help us make our honey.
We can pay you with a sticky treat
because we have no money.
Bee a bug detective. _____

Answer: bees

I come from cocoons
so cozy and tight.
And when it gets dark,
I flutter near light.
Bee a bug detective. _____

Answer: moth

My front and back look quite the same.
I wiggle all around.
You'll find me in the garden
digging tunnels underground.
Bee a bug detective. _____

Answer: worm

I spin a web.
I lay some eggs.
I walk around
on eight thin legs.
Bee a bug detective. _____

Answer: spider

I have a lot of little feet
that I have never stopped to count.
They say I have 100 legs.
Now that is quite a large amount!
Bee a bug detective. _____

Answer: centipede

Which Pet Do You Pick?

I swim in water all day long.
You feed me little flakes.
If I were wild and not a pet,
I'd live in streams and lakes.
Pick a pet. _____

Answer: fish

They say that I have nine long lives.
I land on four soft feet.
I purr and purr when I am rubbed.
The sound is really neat.
Pick a pet. _____

Answer: cat

When out on a walk,
I yip and I yap,
and when I get tired,
I sleep on your lap.
Pick a pet. _____

Answer: puppy

I've got long ears and a cottontail.
I hop on big back feet.
I wiggle my nose to thank you
when you give me carrot treats.
Pick a pet. _____

Answer: bunny

My tail is long,
my whiskers, too.
I'd like a piece of
cheese from you.
Pick a pet. _____

Answer: mouse

At the Beach: What am I?

I look like a star,
but I'm not in the sky.
I cling to the rocks
when a wave comes by.
I'm a _____.

Answer: sea star/starfish

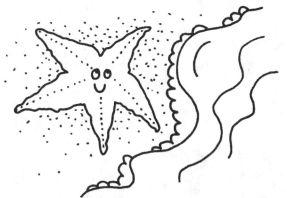

Inside my shells
there is a pearl
for any lucky
boy or girl.
I'm an _____.

Answer: oyster

Do not spend me
at the store.
I'm a dollar you find
when you explore.
I'm a _____.

Answer: sand dollar

Whenever I want to
switch my shell,
another's shell
will do quite well.
I'm a _____.

Answer: hermit crab

Who's in the Ocean?

I'm a fish with fins—
gray, white, or dark.
I've got rows of teeth.
I'm an ocean _____.

Answer: shark

My flippers help me
find a meal.
I swim and bark.
I'm an ocean _____.

Answer: seal

I squirt out my ink.
I'm a sourpuss.
I come with eight legs.
I'm an _____.

Answer: octopus

If you're into large beaks,
then I'm the one.
I fish in the ocean
I'm a _____.

Answer: pelican

What Can You Find in the Classroom?

I have 2 hands. I have a face.
My hands go round and round.
I have the numbers 1 to 12
instead of smiles and frowns.
Find me in the classroom. _____

Answer: clock

I have four legs.
I'm made from a tree.
You stuff your books
inside of me.
Find me in the classroom. _____

Answer: desk

I'm a yellow fellow with a pointed head.
I'm thin as thin can be.
But I leave a trail on a blank white page
when someone writes with me.
Find me in the classroom. _____

Answer: pencil

I'm covered with lines,
and I'm most often white.
I'm handy when
you want to write.
Find me in the classroom. _____

Answer: paper

I take your books from home to school.
I'm red or blue or green or black.
You zip my zippers here and there.
I'm always riding piggyback.
Find me in the classroom. _____

Answer: backpack

I'm rainbow colors
like red and blue.
When you draw or color,
I'm what you use.
Find me in the classroom. _____

Answer: crayons

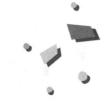

What Am I Playing?

Over my head
and under my feet.
The rope twirls around,
as I jump to the beat.
What am I doing? _____

Answer: jumping rope

I climb the ladder
and then sit down.
Whoosh! I'm swishing
to the ground!
What am I doing? _____

Answer: sliding on the slide

Draw the squares
in white or black.
Throw a stone.
Hop up and back.
What am I doing? _____

Answer: playing hopscotch

I'm "It." I chase you—
one, two, three.
I try to catch
the friends I see.
What am I doing? _____

Answer: playing tag

Balls: Which Sport?

Swoosh!
It's going through the hoop.
The happy crowd
lets out a whoop.
It's a _____.

Answer: basketball

Home run,
single, double, too.
You hit this ball
and catch it, too.
It's a _____.

Answer: baseball

You use a racquet
to hit this ball.
It's yellow or white,
and it's fuzzy and small.
It's a _____.

Answer: tennis ball

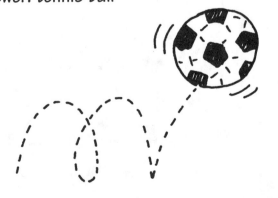

This ball is made of leather—
partly white and partly black.
You try to get it in the goal.
You kick it up and back.
It's a _____.

Answer: soccer ball

Who's Hatching?

A reptile's
hatching out today.
She has big jaws
and starts with A.
Who's hatching? _____

Answer: alligator

A light blue egg
in a cozy, little nest—
out comes a bird
with red on its chest.
Who's hatching? _____

Answer: robin

This reptile is breaking
her egg with a crack.
She hides in the shell
that she wears on her back.
Who's hatching? _____

Answer: turtle

A little baby's hatching out
who's covered all in yellow.
He's peeping and he's cheeping.
He's a little, feathered fellow.
Who's hatching? _____

Answer: chick

They are skinny and long,
curled up in their eggs.
Then they slither right out
with no arms and no legs.
Who's hatching? _____

Answer: snakes

These creatures used to rule the earth.
They hatched from giant eggs.
They all had different sizes
for their tails and heads and legs.
Who's hatching? _____

Answer: dinosaurs

If You Met This Dinosaur, How Would You Greet It?

Its brain is the size of a walnut
in a head that's very small.
Its back is filled with lots of plates
that stand up sharp and tall.
Hello, S_____.

Answer: Stegosaurus

It's the largest dinosaur of all.
Its neck is very long.
You'd run as fast as your legs could go
if this one came along.
Good-bye, Br_____.

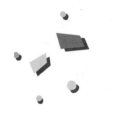

Answer: Brachiosaurus

With two sharp horns
and a fancy collar,
this dinosaur
could make you holler.
Hello, Tr_____.

Answer: Triceratops

The fiercest of the dinosaurs
has strong back legs and feet.
It uses a mouthful of very sharp teeth
to tear and eat its meat.
Good-bye, T_____.

Answer: Tyrannosaurus rex

Who's in the Rain Forest?

When I'm eating my ants,
I couldn't be neater.
I use my long tongue.
I'm a giant _____.

Answer: anteater

I have very long fur,
except on my nose.
I'm the slowest of beasts.
I'm a _____ with three toes.

Answer: sloth

With a giant-sized beak,
and a tail like a fan,
I've got bright-colored feathers.
I'm called a_____.

Answer: toucan

Watch me swinging through the trees.
They say I'm very spunky.
See me hanging by my tail.
I'm a forest spider _____.

Answer: monkey

I have two very bulgy eyes.
I live in trees and logs.
You see me hop, you hear me croak.
I am a spotted _____.

Answer: frog

I am 15 feet long.
No sound do I make.
I've got a forked tongue.
I'm an anaconda _____.

Answer: snake

When I leave my cocoon,
I go fluttering by.
My wings are like jewels.
I'm a _____.

Answer: butterfly

I'm fast and I'm sleek.
I'm a rain-forest star.
My spots make me handsome.
I'm called a _____.

Answer: jaguar

Which Season?

In _____,
trees are nice and bare,
and pretty snowflakes fill the sky.
We like to build in the snow all day
We like the _____, you and I.
Which season?

Answer: winter

In _____
trees are full and green,
and bright, hot sunshine fills the sky.
We like to swim and splash all day.
We like the _____, you and I.
Which season?

Answer: summer

In _____time
trees have brand new leaves
and baby birds fly in the sky.
We like to dig and plant all day.
We like the _____ time, you and I.
Which season?

Answer: spring

In _____,
trees are orange and red,
and leaves are twirling in the sky.
We like to jump in the leaves all day.
We like the _____, you and I.
Which season?

Answer: autumn/fall

Generic Poetry Frame:

In winter, *(change the season name)*
trees _____.
and _____ sky.
We like to _____ all day.
We like the winter, you and I.
(change the season name)

Answers will vary.

• **Variation:** Once the children have guessed all the names of the seasons, make a new activity.
Fill in the seasons, and have the children fill in the blanks of the generic poetry frame above.

Which Month of the Year?

There's always a month of the year
when Martin Luther King Day is here.
It's number one.
We have wintry fun.
Come and whisper the month in my ear.

Answer: January

There's always a month of the year
when Valentine's Day is here.
It's number two.
There's a heart just for you!
Come and whisper the month in my ear.

Answer: February

There's always a month of the year
when St. Patrick's Day is here.
It's number three.
You have to wear green!
Come and whisper the month in my ear.

Answer: March

There's always a month of the year
when the beginning of spring is here.
It's number four.
There are tulips and more.
Come and whisper the month in my ear.

Answer: April

There's always a month of the year
when Memorial Day is here.
It's number five.
Bees buzz in their hive.
Come and whisper the month in my ear.

Answer: May

There's always a month of the year
when the end of school is here.
It's number six.
Time for picnics.
Come and whisper the month in my ear.

Answer: June

There's always a month of the year
when the fireworks show is here.
It's number seven.
It's summer heaven.
Come and whisper the month in my ear.

Answer: July

There's always a month of the year
when the last month of summer is here.
It's number eight.
The weather's great.
Come and whisper the month in my ear.

Answer: August

There's always a month of the year
when the beginning of school is here.
It's number nine.
The classrooms shine.
Come and whisper the month in my ear.

Answer: September

There's always a month of the year
when Halloween is here.
It's number ten.
We dress up again.
Come and whisper the month in my ear.

Answer: October

There's always a month of the year
when Thanksgiving Day is here.
It's number eleven.
The turkey is heaven.
Come and whisper the month in my ear.

Answer: November

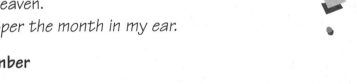

There's always a month of the year
when gift-giving time is here.
It's number twelve.
There are candles and elves.
Come and whisper the month in my ear.

Answer: December

Which Day of the Week?

I picked a day—
a day of the week.
I'll give you a clue,
for each is unique.

Answers will vary.

Clues for You:

It's the first day of the school week. _____
Answer: Monday

It's the middle of the week and has the longest name. _____
Answer: Wednesday

It's the last day of the school week. _____
Answer: Friday

It has seven letters, and it comes after Monday. _____
Answer: Tuesday

It's the day before Friday. _____
Answer: Thursday

It's the first day you can sleep late and play all day. _____
Answer: Saturday

It's the last day of the weekend. _____
Answer: Sunday

Which Holiday?

Black and orange are the colors we use
on this happy holiday.
Can you guess the day I'm thinking of?
You're right! It's _____ Day.

Answer: Halloween

Green and white are the colors we use
on this happy holiday.
Can you guess the day I'm thinking of?
You're right! It's _____ Day.

Answer: St. Patrick's

Red and pink are the colors we use
on this happy holiday.
Can you guess the day I'm thinking of?
You're right! It's _____ Day.

Answer: Valentine's

Red, white, and blue are the colors this day,
and there's a reason why.
Can you guess the day I'm thinking of?
You're right. It's the _____.

Answer: Fourth of July

Resources for Riddles

ABC Animal Riddles by Susan Joyce. Peel Productions, 1999.

Calculator Riddles by David A. Alder. Holiday House, 1996.

Clifford's Riddles by Norman Bridwell. Scholastic Trade, 1990.

Creepy Riddles by Katy Hall and Lisa Einsenberg. Dial Books for Young Readers, 1998.

Eight Ate a Feast of Homonym Riddles by Marvin Terban. Houghton Mifflin Co., 1982.

I Spy School Days: A Book of Picture Riddle by Jean Marzollo. Scholastic, 1995.

Kindle Me a Riddle: A Pioneer Story by Roberta Karim. Greenwillow, 1999.

Lightning Inside You: And Other Native American Riddles by John Bierhorst. William Morrow & Company, 1992.

Playing Possum: Riddles About Kangaroos, Koalas, and Other Marsupials (You Must Be Joking) by John Jansen. Lerner Publications Co., 1995.

The House With No Door: African Riddle-Poems by Brian Swann. Browndeer Press, 1998.

Weather or Not: Riddles About Rain and Shine by Rick Walton. Lerner Publications Co., 1991.

Check Out These Riddle Websites!

http://teacher.Scholastic.com/annie — Discover the Daily Riddle. Help kids build vocabulary, exercise critical-thinking skills, and develop phonemic awareness in this fun rhyming riddle game.

http://www.nwf.org/kids/ — Visit the National Wildlife Federation to read Ranger Rick's Riddle Picks!

http://Scholastic.com/ispy/make/mak.htm — Make Your Own I-Spy! Books and software by Jean Marzollo and Walter Wick.

http://Scholastic.com/magicschoolbus/games/riddle.htm — Discover the Magic School Bus Riddle of the Week!

Notes

Notes

Notes